Models of Salvation

A Biblical Study of Salvation

Copyright © 2013

William (Bill) R. Chambers

You may contact the author through the following:

Mail: Bill Chambers
     115 Lazarus Dr
     Hiram, Ga 30141

Phone: 770 530 -2308
E-mail: billc41@comcast.net

Table of Contents

Chapter One

The Beginning

In a small Georgia town on a hot July night in 1953, I was an eleven year old boy sitting in my usual spot next to an open window in an old Baptist church listening to the crickets chirp and hoping for a cool breeze. The building was typical of most churches in the rural south those days; white with large windows on each side and a tall steeple with a bell inside that was rung every Sunday Morning.

The church was holding its annual summer revival and the preacher, a guest evangelist, was preaching one of those "hellfire and brimstone" sermons that were often heard in those days meant to frighten sinners sufficiently that they would respond to the call for repentance. It's been more than sixty years now and I still remember the title of the sermon, "When Thousands Die in a Moment." Even though I remember the title, somehow I can't recall much of anything said in the sermon.

But at the close of his sermon, as was the custom in those revival meetings, I remember the preacher came down from the pulpit and urged lost sinners to come down and invite Jesus into their hearts and be "saved." As he made his plea, the congregation stood singing a familiar old invitational hymn, "Just as I Am." You might be familiar with the words, "Just as I am, without one plea, but that thy blood was shed for me."

As the congregation was standing and singing, I too, was standing but I wasn't singing. To be honest, I really didn't want to be there, my parents made me go to church every time the doors opened and I hated it. To me church was boring and irrelevant and most of the time I spent there was spent day dreaming about other things. With that kind of attitude, one would wonder why I did what I did that night. The preacher, pleading with sinners to come forward, began walking down the aisle next to my row of pews. As I watched him coming down the aisle he looked over at me and said, "Young man, wouldn't you like to be saved?" And I remember thinking, well, yes; yes I would like to be saved!

Though I had hated going to church, being raised in a Christian home and regularly attending church, I had heard enough about hell and God's anger with sinners to know that one day I needed to do something about that. Nobody wanted to go to hell and for years I had a black cloud hanging over me reminding me that if something didn't change that's where I was going! That fear is what moved me to step out into the aisle where the preacher then led me to the steps of the altar. There we knelt down and he began asking me questions.

"Young man, do you know God loves you? Do you believe that He sent His Son to die on the cross for you? Do you believe that Jesus died so God would forgive you of your sin?" And believing all that was true I answered, "yes I do." And then tears began to fill my eyes as he asked, "Can you see Jesus on the cross bleeding and suffering for your sin?" I remember seeing that vividly in my mind. I envisioned Jesus suffering the agony of crucifixion for me, and as I did it all became very real. At that moment, there were no excuses, there was no doubt - I was convicted of my sinfulness and need of the Savior.

Finally the preacher asked, "Son, do you believe with all your heart that because Jesus died for you that God has forgiven you of all your sin?" Will you accept Him as your Savior tonight and be saved? Believing all that was true I replied "Yes I will."

As I felt the impact of what I had just confessed a sudden peace came over me, a feeling I have never experienced before. We then stood up, and the preacher with his hand on my shoulder, announced to the congregation, "Tonight this young man has accepted the Lord as his personal savior, tonight he has been saved by

God's grace." It was then I noticed my mother had come up during the altar call to the front row where she had been kneeling, weeping and praying that her children would be saved that night. She was so happy when she saw me standing there with the preacher who now had me confess before the church that I had just gave my life to the Lord.

I will never forget as I walked home that summer night, I looked up into the starry sky and thought about what God had done for me. I was forgiven! I was saved! I felt such a weight had been lifted from me. Rather than having that black cloud of fear hanging over me, that night I was on cloud nine. I felt so wonderful and free, I don't know that I have ever felt quite that way since. There can be no doubt, I had a life changing experience that night, an experience that has impacted me even to this day. Any time I re-live that night, I have deep stirrings in my heart and sometimes I get teary eyed. It was so wonderful. To this day I have no misgivings or doubts, I experienced conversion that night, I was truly "born again."

One evening shortly after the revival was over our local pastor came to visit us in our home. The whole family had gathered in the living room, mom, dad and my two younger sisters, one of whom was also saved during the revival. Our pastor gave my sister and I each a new

Schofield Reference Bible as a gift and talked to us about what it meant to be saved. He told us that our salvation was irreversible. There wasn't anything anyone could do to change it. Just as our dad was our earthly father, and nothing could change that, now God was our Heavenly Father and nothing could ever change that. We were eternally secure. This is what some Christians refer to as "once saved, always saved."

Our pastor warned us about legalism, trying to work our way to heaven by keeping the commandments. He said the Ten Commandments were a good guide to live by, but we were now "under grace," we were "free from the law" and all our sin was forgiven for all time, past, present, and future. Of course we needed to be good Christians, but when we did sin now, we wouldn't be lost again, we would still go to heaven, we just wouldn't get the rewards we would have otherwise. But nothing we could do would cause us to be lost! We were heaven bound, guaranteed entrance into the kingdom. I thought, wow! What more could a person ask for?

As I grew older and began making more of my own decisions about how I would live my life, the things the pastor had told me that night continued to have an impact. When faced with decisions regarding the temptations that all young people have, like drinking, sex, foul language, disrespecting my parents, lying and stealing, it was easy for me to give in to something I really wanted to do even if I knew it was wrong. I reasoned as many do, that after all, God knows how weak we are and that no one can live without sin. And besides, all my sins were forgiven, my salvation was secure, no need to worry.

Sometimes when tempted, I thought of some of the biblical heroes like David, Samson and others who drank wine, had numerous wives and concubines too, and did some other questionable things. I used their example as a reason to excuse and justify my partaking of forbidden things.

I remember one night a friend and I were sitting in a car drinking. Both of us having had too much to drink, we were like "three sheets in the wind" as they used to say. You may be aware of how some drunks talk and babble on and on. That was us. As we talked, the conversation somehow turned to the topic of religion. I remember us talking about how that if Jesus were to come that night we would be gloriously raptured up to heaven. Never mind that neither of us had been to church, opened a Bible, or prayed in years. In fact, the last time I remembered praying was when a jealous husband was chasing me with his shotgun because I had been with his wife! I was praying for deliverance that night!

Regrettably, I spent many years of my adult life like that, and all the while believing I was saved, that my salvation was secure because of what I had been taught in church as a boy. Now at this point I know some people would be quick to say, well, you weren't really saved or you wouldn't have done those things. And at first that thought seems logical, but then, is it realistic? There are stories similar to mine that could be told by untold numbers of people. I personally know many people who were "saved," but later in life when temptations, and / or trials came their way they drifted back into a life of open sin. But they weren't really troubled by that because they had been taught, just as I had, that it was impossible for them to lose their salvation.

I remember attending the funeral of a close relative who was saved when he was a young man, but whom I personally know lived a very sinful life. One afternoon He died in his sleep of a sudden heart attack. I had spoken to him that morning about our plans to go hunting that afternoon. We had no idea that he would die in his sleep later that day as he napped on his sofa. I knew he had never turned back to the Lord and so did the preacher who spoke at his funeral. And yet knowing this, the preacher told the congregation, "Yes, we know that this man lived a sinful life, but back when he was a young man he gave his heart to the Lord and was saved. Therefore we know that he is now in heaven being reunited with his family members who have gone on before." This was only one of many similar funeral sermons I heard over the years.

So regardless if someone says, if a person were really saved they wouldn't do those things, the truth is, that for millions of Christians the foundation of their faith rests on the premise that once a person believes and accepts Jesus as their Savior they cannot be lost – no matter how they live, and many are left with a false security rather than an eternal security.

As I grew older and began to study the Bible for myself, I began to be troubled by a number of texts in the Bible that seem to contradict the "once saved, always saved" teaching. One such example is found in Colossians 1:21 - 23 which says -

"And you, who once were alienated and enemies in your mind by wicked works, yet now He has reconciled in the body of His flesh through death, to present you holy, and blameless, and above reproach in His sight - ***if indeed you continue in the faith, grounded and steadfast, and are not***

moved away from the hope of the gospel which you heard, *which was preached to every creature under heaven, of which I, Paul, became a minister."*

Do not overlook the word "if." *"**If you continue** in the faith grounded, and steadfast."* The word *"if"* implies that salvation is conditional depending upon our **continued** faithfulness. The word *"continue"* in this text is translated from the Greek word "epimeno" which means "to stay with," "to remain," or "to persevere." There can be no question as to what Paul is saying here, if we hope to be saved, we must day by day, continue a meaningful relationship with Christ. There are many other similar passages as well, but I will not take the space to list them here.

Having said that, I realize there are those who would interpret them in a way that may produce a different conclusion. Which prompts the question - Is it possible that all the Bible Colleges, theological seminaries, preachers and Christians who believe and teach that a person cannot lose his or her salvation for any reason could be wrong?

It seems that every church denomination, including the non-denominational groups, each have their own unique teaching about salvation, what it means and how a person obtains it. The problem is that all of them cannot be right, and that is a serious problem!

We know this is true of numerous other teachings as well. Most all of us have heard, or been involved in debates about issues such as life after death, the rapture, the tribulation, the Trinity, the list goes on and on. I will not take the time to investigate these kinds of issues because many of them are not necessarily "life and death" issues. However personal salvation is, so the focus of this book will be on that topic.

I am aware that some may be tempted to close this book right now thinking - I don't need to study salvation, I know all about that. But before you do, ask yourself, honestly – Am I absolutely sure that I know beyond a shadow of doubt the truth about what salvation is and that I have experienced it for myself?

Personal salvation, because it is a life and death issue is far too important to get wrong. It is far too important to treat lightly or haphazardly. It is far too important to trust to someone else; whether that person be a Rabbi, a Priest, a Protestant Preacher, or even one's parents. It is not safe to put our salvation in another's hands! We need to know what salvation is, and experience it for ourselves. I want to repeat that with emphasis. *We need to know what salvation is, and experience it for ourselves!!*

So, how do we accomplish this? How can we know and experience salvation for ourselves and know that we are right? And the answer to that question can be found in only one place, and that is the Bible. I do not know the source of the following quotation, but it expresses what our attitude towards this question must be if we are to find the truth:

"What says the Bible, the precious Bible, this my only question be. The teachings of men so often mislead us, what says the Bible to me?"

Notice the words *"What says the Bible to me?"* Not what it says to the teacher or to the preacher, but to me! The Bible, not the church, not the seminary, not the preacher, not even mom and dad, but the Bible only, is where we must find the truth about salvation, period!

Today we live in an age in which all of us are educated, at least to the point that with few exceptions that everyone can read and write. We have the free time to research and study; we have countless books, and now computers and the internet with which we have a world of information at our fingertips. We have Bible study tools such as concordances, commentaries, Hebrew and Greek lexicons and dictionaries, user friendly computer programs, and instructional guides that teach us how to study the Bible. If we take advantage of all these things we can practically become biblical scholars. For most of us there is no excuse for being ignorant in regards to what the Bible teaches. It is my hope that this book will be another tool to help you better understand, and, if you have not already, encourage you to experience salvation for yourself. So please, read on.

Chapter Two

About Metaphors and Models

We begin our study of salvation by defining the word "salvation" itself. We need to know exactly what the word salvation means and its proper use, not only in English, but more importantly in the original languages of the Bible, the Hebrew and Greek. Unfortunately many biblical words have taken on meanings never intended by the writers of Scripture thus making it critical that we make an effort to find out what the original writer of the text wanted to say. Word studies can be very helpful to us in accomplishing that task.

The English language dictionary I will use is the Shorter Oxford English Dictionary. It gives two defintions for the word "salvation." The first one is listed as "christian theological" and is as follows: *The saving of the soul; deliverance from sin and its consequences and admission into eternal life, brought about by Christ.*

The second definition is listed as "general," and is as follows: *The action of saving something; the state of being saved; preservation or deliverance from destruction, ruin, loss, or harm.*

Of course the "christian theological" definition would appear to be accurate to most Christians. But actually, the "general" definition, as we will see, is closer to the definition of the words translated "salvation" in the biblical languages. Actually the word "salvation" is a Latin word from the thirteenth century chosen by the translaters of the King James Bible in AD 1611 to translate the Old Testament Hebrew word "yeshu'ah" and the New Testament Greek word "soteria." Both of these words are nouns which mean: *"deliverance, preservation or healing."* This is similar to the general definition of salvation given in the English dictionary.

Once we are clear on the basic meaning of the biblical word for salvation, the next logical step would be to consider what it is we are seeking deliverance, preservation or healing from, in order to best understand the method and experience of salvation itself. Depending on one's situation, that could be any number of things. For example, I was seeking to be saved, or deliverance from that jealous husband with his shotgun that night I mentioned in the last chapter.

But in this study we are concerned only with the condition in which all mankind finds itself and that is being mortal, being subject to death. It is clear that sooner or later we all die and that thought is terrifying for most of us. Every human being, good or bad, with few exceptions, either has or will experience death.

The Bible refers to this death more than fifty times as *"sleep."* David called it the *"sleep of death"* (Psalm 13:3). But the Scriptures go on to say that those who sleep the sleep of death will *"awake,"* meaning they will be raised to life again.

"And many of those who sleep in the dust of the earth shall awake, Some to everlasting life, Some to shame and everlasting contempt." (Daniel 12:2)

Jesus confirms this in the Gospel of John -

*"Do not marvel at this; for the hour is coming in which **all who are in the graves** will hear His voice and come forth-- those who have done good, to the resurrection of life, and those who have done evil, to the resurrection of condemnation."* (John 5:28,29)

Jesus says *"all that in the graves...shall come forth,"* some raised *"to the resurrection of life,"* and others *"to the resurrection of condemnation."* Those resurrected in the second group, at the end of the *"great white throne"* judgment, will die again in what the Bible calls the *"second death"* (Revelation 20:11 - 15). Some teach that the second death is really *"hell,"* a place where sinners go and burn forever. But why would the Bible call it death if people are alive and conscious even though they are in torment? It would seem logical that this death is called the second death because, unlike the first death, the second death is an eternal, everlasting cessation of life. But regardless of whether this is believed to be a place of eternal torment or an eternal death, this death is what we want to be "saved" from.

I have read that the strongest instinct we humans posses is the desire to live. No one in their right mind wants to die. Never mind heaven with its streets of gold and beautiful mansions; that is only a fringe benefit many people couldn't care less about. Who really wants a golden crown with stars in it anyway? Never mind the rewards - for the most of us, our major concern is just to live! But the Bible tells us that only God inherently possesses immortality –

*"Which He (Christ) will manifest in His own time, He who is the blessed and only Potentate, the King of kings and Lord of lords, **who alone has immortality**..."*

(I Timothy 6:15,16)

But even though God is the only One to inherently possess immortality, we can have it too and the Bible says we do well to seek for it –

"God, who "will render to each one according to his deeds": eternal life to those who by patient continuance in doing good seek for glory, honor, and immortality;

(Romans 2:6,7)

The Bible also tells us, as we read earlier, that the righteous, *"who by continuance in well doing,"* whether they sleep in the grave or live until the second coming of Christ, will, at that time receive immortality –

*"For since by man came death, by Man also came the resurrection of the dead. For as in Adam all die, **even so in Christ all shall be made alive. But each one in his own order: Christ the firstfruits, afterward those who are Christ's at His coming."***   (I Corinthians 15:21 - 23)

*"In a moment, in the twinkling of an eye, at the last trumpet. For the trumpet will sound, and the dead will be raised incorruptible, and we shall be changed. For this corruptible must put on incorruption, and **this mortal must put on immortality."***   (I Corinthians 15:52,53)

Some people are very confident that they possess eternal life. Some are not sure as to whether or not they have it and some know they are "lost" and without any hope for life beyond death. And still others have a false assurance - They believe they will, when the truth is they will not. But whichever category we may fit into, let us press on to seek for immortality, eternal life, the gift freely offered us by a loving God.

So how can we be sure that we obtain salvation from sin and its deadly consequence? Before we begin to attempt to answer that, consider the thoughtful statement found in "The Desire of Ages," pg 494 -

"The plan of redemption is so far-reaching that philosophy cannot explain it. It will ever remain a mystery that the most profound reasoning cannot fathom. The science of salvation cannot be explained; but it can be known by experience."

This basically says that the science, or the knowledge of salvation is something that can't be put into words but must be experienced. That's true of many things in life isn't it? An example would be the taste of a certain food, like a banana. When we eat a banana, we know what it is like to experience the taste. But we don't know how to put that taste onto words so that we could tell someone else exactly what a banana tastes like. The only way they could know would be to bite into the banana and experience the taste for themselves.

Since the science of salvation is something that can't be put into words but must be experienced, then we need things like metaphors, allegories, and stories to give us some idea of what the experience is like. The Scriptures provide these kinds of helps, some of which we will examine, but as we do, we do well to remember that all of them have their limitations and we must be careful that we don't push them beyond those limits. Parables, metaphors and models are often used in Scripture to illustrate the experience of salvation. I prefer to use the word "model" which is defined as, *"a description or analogy used to help visualize something that cannot be directly observed."*

We will examine three models of the plan of salvation in this book. 1) Legal Model, 2) Deliverance Model and 3) Healing Model. As we examine each model there are three basic things we want to consider:

1) Is it biblical? Remember, "What says the Bible?"
2) How is sin defined in this model?
3) How does this model work and what is its focus?

As we will see, each model will have a different focus and corresponding method of bringing about salvation. And because God graciously meets people where they are, we will see that each model can have a place in the experience of salvation depending on where a person may be in their own spiritual journey.

In the next chapter we will examine the legal model. We examine it first because for most Christians it is a primary or beginning model and as such the one most people are familiar with.

Chapter Three
The Legal Model

In this chapter we will examine the legal model of the plan of salvation. As I mentioned in the last chapter, we begin with it because it is the one most people are introduced to as an illustration of salvation or how a person is "saved." It is an elementary, or beginning model, which for centuries has been widely taught and accepted in the Christian church.

I refer to this model as "legal" because it is based on a system of authority, law and punishment. In the legal system a powerful authority establishes laws for others to live by and in order to make these laws effective there is an imposed penalty for disobedience. Anyone found guilty of violating the law can only avoid the penalty if forgiven or pardoned by the authority. This is accepted by human societies as a basic premise for life in this world; otherwise life on this planet would be "survival of the fittest" with the strong and the cruel taking advantage of everyone else.

Every world government operates on this premise. The government is the authority which legislate laws and imposes penalties upon law breakers. We see this concept in other institutions as well, like the military and the companies we work for. We also see it in the family where the parents are the authority who make the rules and impose the punishment upon the children as they see fit. All of this is a normal part of life in this world.

At the same time, it is apparent that the majority of people see God, either the God of the Bible or some other god, whether or not they actually worship Him, as the ultimate authority who rightfully makes laws and metes out punishment to the inhabitants of this world as He sees fit. And of course there are those who deny the existence of any god, those who are their own moral authority and therefore recognize no rules or penalties other than those imposed by human authorities.

But our study will be only concerned with the God of the Bible beginning with our first question is: Is the legal model biblical? Do we find this model in the Scriptures? My answer is yes. But, I need to qualify that in that, when God chooses to use the legal method or model with its laws and punishments, it is out of necessity and not His preferred method. Let me explain -

The Bible tells us that God is the Almighty Sovereign Creator of all things in heaven and earth and as such He is the Supreme Authority of the entire universe and has the right to run it any way He chooses. But, at the same time, the Bible says *"God is love"* and love cannot exist for long in forced or robotic relationships. If God "programmed" us to love Him and do right we would be no more than mere robots. So God chooses, actually He insists, on the freedom of all His creatures.

The Bible tells us soon after God created the earth, most of His earthly children, being free, rebelled against Him going their own way wanting nothing to do with Him. The few who did remain loyal, the Israelites, ended up in Egypt where many of them became involved in the worship of the pagan gods of Egypt and forgot much of what they had known of the God of their forefathers. The Israelites eventually became slaves to the Egyptians and in their affliction cried out to God for deliverance. God heard their cries and sent Moses to bring them out. Notice how the Lord speaks of them as recorded in the book of Hosea -

"When Israel was a child, I loved him, And out of Egypt I called My son. As they called them, So they went from them; They sacrificed to the Baals, And burned incense to carved images."   (Hosea 11:1,2)

"When Israel was a child" - God likened them to children and goes on to speak of how He fed them, taught them to walk and cared for them even though they were continually

25

going after other gods. They were like strong willed, rebellious children, determined to go their own destructive way in spite of all that God could do. With this kind of language and illustrations, one could see this as a "parent / child" model.

After leaving Egypt, it became clear how rebellious the Israelites had become. Moses had a terrible time with them and eventually, for their best good, God had to "lay down the law" with threats of punishment to get their attention. The Bible gives us the principle that applies to this situation.

"Knowing this: that the law is not made for a righteous person, but for the lawless and insubordinate, for the ungodly and for sinners, for the unholy and profane, for murderers of fathers and murderers of mothers, for manslayers..." (I Timothy 1:9)

If the Israelites had been a humble people, unselfishly loving God and one another, there would have been no need for God to give them commandments and laws. But, the Bible says they were *"stiff-necked."* The Hebrew word from which that is translated means that they were *"obstinate, cruel and rebellious."* God, in order to keep them in line until such time as they were willing to listen to

Him, had to establish a system of laws and punishment. And just as a good parent, even though it was unpleasant for Him, there were times when God had to carry out those threats. For their own good they needed to "fear Him," to see Him as One not to be trifled with, and that He meant what He said!

I can now look back and see this principle at work in my own childhood. There were times when I didn't see the sense of doing, or not doing, some of the things my parents said. When I "tested the waters" so to speak, and ignored or disobeyed their rules it resulted with a painful penalty. Sometimes I was hurt by the very thing they had warned me of and sometimes I was hurt by my dad's leather belt as it stuck my hinder parts. In either case, I learned that in life there are painful consequences to certain actions and attitudes.

I remember there were times I pushed my mother (who was more tolerant than my dad) to her limit and in her frustration with me she would yell, "if you don't stop that, I'm going to skin you alive!" Maybe you have been threatened in similar way by your parents. But I knew not to take it literally, she would never do a thing like that, but, I also knew it was at this point I had better pay attention, I had better stop or I would have to face my dad when he got home! Yet in all this, whether it was my mother or my dad, I always knew that they loved me and only wanted my best good. And when I realized I had done wrong and went to them expressing my sorrow and guilt, forgiveness freely followed without fail.

I believe that this is similar to the way it is with our Heavenly Father as well. The stories in the Old Testament demonstrate that God, just as the loving parent, cares enough about His children to teach and to warn. And when they won't listen and do things that are damaging to themselves and others, God cares enough to threaten and at appropriate times see that they are punished for their own best good. And when the rebellious child comes to his senses, realizing he's done wrong, comes to God burdened with remorse and guilt, God freely forgives him and treats him as if he had never sinned! When he senses God's forgiveness, he feels relieved, refreshed and everything is right again. The relationship is restored and ultimately the restored relationship is what God really wants in all this. Once the relationship is restored, God can continue to work in the child's life helping him grow to maturity.

But as I mentioned at the opening of this chapter this is a "beginning" model. As we become more experienced and knowledgeable in life we should be led to a more advanced model. For example, my parents had the hope that as I grew older, that I would come to the place that they would not have to "lay down the law" anymore. That the time would come when they would not have to make threats or punish me anymore. That I would eventually grow up to be a mature and responsible adult who no longer did those things that called for punishment and asking forgiveness. That I would understand why the discipline was needed and through it all, that they wanted only my best good. And finally the time would come that I would no longer "fear" them as a child, but love and respect them as an adult.

In the same way, God wants all His children to grow up too. To come to the place where they do not need the Ten Commandments hanging on the wall or threats of punishment ringing in their ears to keep them from misbehaving. That they would eventually grow up to be mature, humble, loving and compassionate adults, grown-ups who have come to *"love God with all their heart and their neighbor as themselves."* (Matthew 22:37). As I stated previously, one could almost see this as a "parent / child" model though I hesitate to use that as a model because many of those parent / child relationships can be abusive and therefore not very useful to those who have experienced that kind of abuse as children.

Nevertheless, what we have described is the ideal for the legal model. Unfortunately, instead of the beginning model it should be, the legal model has come to be the dominant, and for most, the only model. It has been pushed far beyond its limits as a useful metaphor for salvation. It has developed into a complex "forensic" model. Forensic is defined as: *"pertaining to courts of justice, or relating to or used in legal proceedings."* In other words the legal model, instead of being patterned after a loving parent - child relationship, is now patterned after the modern day court system of justice we find in the Western World.

While there are many variations, basically God, instead of our loving heavenly Father, is seen as the Judge and Executioner, Jesus is seen as an Advocate or lawyer, Satan as an accuser or prosecutor and the sinner as a condemned criminal. A criminal guilty of breaking God's law which is a capital offense. Even though God is a loving and just Judge, He cannot overlook the fact that justice demands that the penalty be imposed on the guilty. The sinner is in big trouble with God!

This is where the plan of salvation comes in. In this "modified" legal model salvation is likened to being pardoned by a judge and the death penalty canceled because someone died the criminals place." At this point someone might recite John 3:16 –

"For God so loved the world that He gave His only begotten Son, that whoever believes in Him should not perish but have everlasting life."

In the legal model that verse is understood to say that God, seeing the hopeless condition of sinners, because He loves them, sent His perfect and sinless Son to pay the penalty for sin in their place. When Jesus died on the cross, that act "justified" God in legally pardoning the guilty sinner. (This is the meaning of "justification," or what it means to be "justified" according to traditional teaching.) But for this arrangement to take effect, one must believe that Christ died for them and accept Him as their personal Savior. The moment they do that, they are forgiven, and being forgiven they are no longer under the sentence of death and will be granted eternal life in heaven! That's all there is to it.

Pretty simple huh? I don't know how many times I have heard someone say "it's so simple a child can understand it." But that is only until you take a closer look and get into some of the details. Then it can become very complex and questions can arise that are very difficult to answer. When that happens, instead of a logical answer, you hear "well, we just have to take that on faith," meaning that no one knows the answer and faith now becomes a "leap in the dark."

As we take a closer look at this modified, modern day legal model, the question is still important – is this biblical? Can we find this in the Bible? This is where I would normally list several verses from the Bible that demonstrate this forensic view of the legal model. But I have read the Bible through several times and in many different versions. I have studied it for untold hours and I have to say that I have found little in the Scriptures that fit this modified legal model of salvation so widely taught and believed in the churches today.

In ancient times in the land of the Bible there was no court system as we know it today for the writers of Scripture to use as a model. The word "court" can be found in the Bible many times, but it is usually referring to an enclosed area, such as the courtyard of the temple, not a court room as we know it today. And even the words *"judge"* and *"judgment"* are not often used in the same way as they are in the legal / court room setting we are so familiar with. Neither can I find in the Bible any thing close to some of the phrases that are so often repeated, like

"Jesus died to pay the penalty for our sin" or "Jesus died so we could be pardoned or forgiven." (I will discuss this in more detail in another chapter.)

While it is true that some books of the Bible do use some legal terminology, much of that is often due to translation rather than inspiration. A word study of the legal terms we find in most English versions of the Bible will quickly reveal this. For example, the word *"advocate"* used in the King James Versions.

"My little children, these things I write to you, so that you may not sin. And if anyone sins, we have an Advocate with the Father, Jesus Christ the righteous."   (I John 2:1)

When we see the word "advocate," most of us immediately think of a lawyer, thus people see Christ as being our lawyer in a heavenly court. But the Greek word from which *"advocate"* is translated is "parakletos," and it simply means *"called to ones aid"* or *"helper."* It is the same word used in John 14:16 where Jesus says:

"And I will pray the Father, and He will give you another Helper, that He may abide with you forever"   (John 14:16)

In this verse, "parakletos" is not translated *"advocate"* but *"Helper."* Here it is not used as a title for Jesus but as a title for the Holy Spirit. The Holy Spirit is to be understood as our helper just as Jesus is also to be seen as our helper, not our lawyer. Neither the Apostle John nor Jesus used this word in a court room setting, nor did they intend for these words to be understood in a legal / forensic context. As I said, it is a matter of translation, not inspiration. No English translation of the Bible is inspired, only the original words written by the prophets were inspired and that's why word studies of the original words are so critical to finding the truth for ourselves.

At this point you might ask - How did this modified version of the legal model become so prominent in the churches? To understand this we need to look at some church history. There are many resources to choose from. The following is a copy of an article I found on the internet site, Wikipedia, that, beginning back in the 13th Century, gives the history of how the legal view or model developed in the church long ago. It is a little long, but worth the time to read if you want to know how this came about.

The Origin of the Legal View of the Atonement -

Thomas Aquinas, (1225 - 1274) was held in the Catholic Church to be the model teacher for those studying for the priesthood. The works for which he is best-known are the

Summma Theologica and the *Summa Contra Gentiles*. As one of the 33 Doctors of the Church, he is considered the Church's greatest theologian and philosopher. Pope Benedict XV declared: "The Church has declared Thomas' doctrines to be her own." Aquinas considers the atonement in the Summa Theologiae, into what is now the standard Catholic understanding of atonement. He wishes to explore the exact nature of sin, debt, punishment, and grace. In his section on man, he considers whether punishment is good and appropriate. He concludes that:

1. punishment is a morally good response to sin
2. "Christ bore a satisfactory punishment, not for His, but for our sins," and
3. substitution for another's sin is entirely possible.

In his section on the Incarnation, Aquinas argues that Christ's death satisfies the penalty owed by sin, and that it was Christ's Passion specifically that was needed to pay the debt of man's sin. For Aquinas, the Passion of Jesus provided the merit needed to pay for sin: "Consequently Christ by His Passion merited salvation, not only for Himself, but likewise for all His members," and that the atonement consisted in Christ's giving to God more "than was required to compensate for the offense of the whole human race." In this way, Aquinas articulated the formal beginning of the idea of a superabundance of merit, which became the basis for the Catholic concept of the Treasury of Merit (Indulgence). Aquinas also articulated the ideas of salvation that are now standard within the Catholic church: that justifying grace is provided through the sacraments; that the condign merit of our actions is matched by Christ's merit from the Treasury of Merit; and that sins can be classified as mortal and venial. For Aquinas, one is saved by drawing on Christ's merit which is provided through the sacraments of the church.

Calvin was the first systematic theologian of the Reformation. As such, he wanted to solve the problem of Christ's atonement in a way that did justice to the Scriptures and Church Fathers, while still rejecting the need for condign merit. His solution was that Christ's death on the cross paid not a general penalty for humanity's sins, but a specific penalty for the sins of individual people. That is, when Jesus died on the cross, his death paid the penalty at that time for the sins of all those who are saved. One obviously necessary feature of this idea is that Christ's atonement is limited in its effect only to those whom God has *chosen* to be saved, since the debt for sins was paid at a particular point in time (at the crucifixion).

For Calvin, this also required drawing on Augustine's earlier theory of predestination. Additionally, in rejecting the idea of penance, Calvin shifted from Aquinas' idea that satisfaction was penance (which focused on satisfaction as a change in humanity), to the idea of satisfying God's wrath. This ideological shift places the focus on a change in God, who is propitiated through Christ's death. The Calvinist understanding of the atonement and satisfaction is penal substitution: Christ is a substitute taking our punishment and thus satisfying the demands of justice and appeasing God's wrath so that God can justly show grace.

It was not until St. Anselm's famous work *Cur Deus Homo* (1098) that attention was focused on the theology of redemption with the aim of providing more exact definitions (though there is disagreement as to how influential penal conceptions were in the first five centuries). Anselm held that to sin is for man "not to render his due to God." Comparing what was due to God and what was due to the feudal Lord, he argued that what was due to God was honour. "'Honour' comprises the whole complex of service and worship which the whole creation, animate and inanimate, in heaven and earth, owes to the Creator. The honour of God is injured by the withdrawal of man's service which he is due to offer." This failure constitutes a debt, weight or doom, for which man must make satisfaction, but which lies beyond his competence; only if a new man can be found who by perfect obedience can satisfy God's honour and by some work of supererogation can provide the means of paying the existing debt of his fellows, can God's original purpose be fulfilled. So Christ not only lives a sinless life, which is again his due, but also is willing to endure death for the sake of love. Thus, Anselm's view can best be understood from medieval feudalistic conceptions of authority, of sanctions and of reparation. Anselmian satisfaction contrasts with penal substitution in that Anselm sees the satisfaction (i.e. restitution) as an alternative to punishment "The honour taken away must be repaid, or punishment must follow" (bk 1 ch 8), whereas penal substitution views the punishment as the means of satisfaction.

Broadly speaking, Martin Luther followed Anselm, thus remaining mainly in the "Latin" model identified by Gustaf Aulén. However, he held that Christ's atoning work encompassed both his active and passive obedience to the law: as the perfectly innocent God-man, he fulfilled the law perfectly during his life and he, in his death on the cross, bore the eternal punishment that all men deserved for their breaking the law. Unlike Anselm, Luther thus combines both satisfaction and punishment.

Calvin appropriated Anselm's ideas but crucially changed the terminology to that of the criminal law with which he was familiar - he was trained as a lawyer - reinterpreted in the light of Biblical teaching on the law. Man is guilty before God's judgment and the only appropriate punishment is eternal death. The Son of God has become man and has stood in man's place to bear the immeasurable weight of wrath; the curse, and the condemnation of a righteous God. He was "made a substitute and a surety in the place of transgressors and even submitted as a criminal, to sustain and suffer all the punishment which would have been inflicted on them."

Sources: *Early Christian Doctrines* (fifth, revised edition; London: Adam & Charles Black, 1977 F. W. Dillistone *The Christian Understanding of the Atonement,* Nisbet 1968 / Wikipedia encyclopedia.

After reading and attempting to grasp all that, it's easy to see that what is said to be "so simple a child can understand it," has been hopelessly complicated by some educated theologians. You may have also noticed that a lot of what these theologians used to base their understanding of salvation on was not the Bible, but those men they revered as "church fathers." And unfortunately this kind of thing continues to this day among far too many church leaders, clergy, and educators. I wonder if they ever heard and seriously considered the words I continue to remind you of, *"What says the Bible, the precious Bible, this my only question be, the teachings of men so often mislead us, what says the Bible to me?"*

Personally, I attribute a lot of the church's use of the forensic / court view to Martin Luther and John Calvin. These men were good men whom God used mightily during the Reformation, and though they re-discovered some truths lost during the Dark Ages, they did not recover them all. Both these men first studied law but later decided to go into the ministry. Both were trained as lawyers, not theologians (As mentioned in the Wikipedia article). During the Reformation period, Calvin wrote a monumental four-volume work entitled, "The Institutes of the Christian Religion." Calvin's teachings contained in these volumes have had an enormous impact on many major church bodies to this day. The doctrine of the immortality of the soul, the eternal suffering of the lost in hellfire, predestination and the law court / forensic view of salvation can all be traced back to Calvin's influence on the

Church through this work. By the way, these volumes are still available today in your local Christian book store!

The King James Version of the Bible was translated in this era as well and its translators were likely influenced by the writings of Calvin and Luther as well. Evidence of that can be seen in the use of many Latin words such as *"justification," "sanctification,"* and *"propitiation."* These words were not the words of the prophets which were originally written in Hebrew or Greek not in Latin. Latin is the language heavily used to this day in the legal profession and preferred by John Calvin. It should come as no surprise that we find a lot of this legal terminology in this popular version of the Bible and thus passed on into Church doctrine.

Though I can't say this forensic / legal model is biblical, it is so deeply rooted in the Church we have to accept it as having a role in modern day Christianity. As I pondered what that role would be I have come to this conclusion: Because so many people are introduced to this model and as a result see God as a fearsome Deity that is angry with sinners and will burn them in hell unless they repent and are forgiven, they need to know that there is pardon readily available and Jesus provides that for them. I am reminded of what the Apostle Paul wrote in Philippians:

"Some indeed preach Christ even from envy and strife, and some also from good will: The former preach Christ from selfish ambition, not sincerely, supposing to add affliction to my chains; but the latter out of love, knowing that I am appointed for the defense of the gospel. What then? Only that in every way, whether in pretense or in truth, Christ is preached; and in this I rejoice, yes, and will rejoice."

(Philippians 1:15 – 18)

Even though this model may not provide the ideal setting, Christ is preached and that is important. God meets people where they are and leads them no faster than they are able to follow. And those of us who have taken the responsibility to teach others "the truth" should be careful we do that as well.

Having said that, we need to be aware of a couple of other problems with this legal plan of salvation as it has developed over the years. The following statement from the earlier internet article is really a summation of what is commonly believed and taught today by most Christians -

"This ideological shift places the focus on a change in God, who is propitiated through Christ's death. The Calvinist understanding of the atonement and satisfaction is penal substitution: Christ is a substitute taking our punishment and thus satisfying the demands of justice and appeasing God's wrath so that God can justly show grace."

Note the legal terminology. God needs to be *"propitiated"* which means He needs to be "appeased." This has come to be understood as the purpose of the death of Christ and the meaning of the "atonement." As stated above - *"Christ as a substitute taking our punishment and thus satisfying the demands of justice and appeasing God's wrath."*

The most critical problem with this view is that it distorts the character of God. No matter how sacred many Christians hold this doctrine, after thoughtful study, one can see that Satan has artfully crafted a theory of salvation that makes God look no better than the King Nebuchadnezzar who said – "If you don't worship me I will have you thrown into the burning fiery furnace!" This model makes God more like the pagan gods of old who must be appeased with a blood sacrifice rather than our loving heavenly Father. It provokes a greater fear of God than the fear of sin itself.

Let's go back to the "parent / child" model for a moment. It doesn't matter how abusive some human parents may be, they would never burn their children to death, let alone burn them forever! The church teaching this kind of thing has made God look like a worse child abuser than any human would ever dream of being! Some, as the Anglican Church recently stated, "Have made God look like a sadistic monster!" (For a detailed biblical study of God's wrath, death, hell and the lake of fire see my "Sure Word Study.") The book "The Great Controversy," Pacific Press Publishing Assoc, contains this sobering statement -

"When we consider in what false colors Satan has painted the character of God, can we wonder that our merciful Creator is feared, dreaded, and even hated? The appalling views of God which have spread over the world from the teachings of the pulpit have made thousands, yes, millions, of skeptics and infidels."

Note the source of this slander, "from the teachings of the pulpit." Think about that. This is where most people learn about God and what He is like. It's not in the bars, at the gym, or in the shopping malls, but in the church! Unfortunately many of us in the ministry have not done a very good job teaching the truth about God's gracious character.

But looking back to the Wikipedia article, besides the legal terminology, I couldn't help but to also notice the words, *"focus on a change in God."* This is in direct contradiction of the words of the Lord himself who said God does not change. Saying that God has to be persuaded to change by the death of a sacrifice places the problem with God and not with us. But the reality is that the change that needs to take place is not with God, but in us! The death of Christ was necessary to change us, to propitiate us, not God! The "atonement" is not to reconcile God back to us, but to reconcile us back to God! God did not leave us, we left Him!

Another problem with the legal model is that there is little, if any, emphasis on the necessity of a change of character or the overcoming of sin. The major focus is on forgiveness, or, to use the legal word, "pardon." But even then, it is not true forgiveness. Most biblical words translated "forgive" or "forgiveness" mean to "let go" or "to release" or "set free" without demanding any retribution, or in the case of a debt, to release one from having to repay the debt. The one doing the forgiving is willing to personally take the loss. Jesus told a story to illustrate this point. This particular story is found in Matthew 18 -

"Therefore the kingdom of heaven is like a certain king who wanted to settle accounts with his servants. And when he had begun to settle accounts, one was brought to him

who owed him ten thousand talents. But as he was not able to pay, his master commanded that he be sold, with his wife and children and all that he had, and that payment be made. The servant therefore fell down before him, saying, 'Master, have patience with me, and I will pay you all.' Then the master of that servant was moved with compassion, released him, and forgave him the debt. But that servant went out and found one of his fellow servants who owed him a hundred denarii; and he laid hands on him and took him by the throat, saying, 'Pay me what you owe!' So his fellow servant fell down at his feet and begged him, saying, 'Have patience with me, and I will pay you all.' And he would not, but went and threw him into prison till he should pay the debt. So when his fellow servants saw what had been done, they were very grieved, and came and told their master all that had been done. Then his master, after he had called him, said to him, 'You wicked servant! I forgave you all that debt because you begged me. Should you not also have had compassion on your fellow servant, just as I had pity on you?' And his master was angry, and delivered him to the torturers until he should pay all that was due to him." (Matthew 18:23 - 34)

Note Jesus makes the point that the lord of this servant freely forgave all his debt. The lord of the servant "let it go," he took the loss, and did not require that he or someone else repay it for him. Jesus is making the point that this is the true meaning of forgiveness. That this is the way we must forgive one another. And would not God forgive us just as freely as He asked us to forgive others? If God would forgive us only if Jesus paid the penalty, then He has not forgiven us at all, He has only accepted payment from someone else. That is not forgiveness! And God's gracious character is again brought into question.

In addition to that, the false assurance that forgiveness is all we need to be "saved" leads to presumption. By presumption I mean that believing we've been forgiven for all our sin for all time, past, present and future, and that "Jesus has done it all, there is nothing for us to do" resulting in our continuing to live the same selfish, sinful life as before and thinking all the time we are "saved." I believe this kind of thinking is the basis for the "once saved - always saved" doctrine I was taught as a boy. Many who believe this, just as I did, often go on their merry way through life rejoicing in their pardon thinking that's all that's needed while there is little, if any, change in the condition of the heart. This makes a mockery of true Christianity!

But remember the night Nicodemus came to Jesus and asked how to be saved? Did Jesus say *"you must be forgiven"*? Or, did He say, *"you must be born again"*? (John 3:7) Simply being forgiven will not save us! Forgiveness does little to change the heart. It will not keep us from doing the same sinful things over and over again! Being forgiven will not make a cruel and untrustworthy person safe to live with! We must have what King David prayed for after his great sin, *"a new heart and a right spirit"* (Psalm 51:10). Add to that what the Apostle John wrote -

"Whoever abides in Him does not sin. Whoever sins has neither seen Him nor known Him. Little children, let no one deceive you. He who practices righteousness is righteous, just as He is righteous. He who sins is of the devil,..."

(I John 3:6 – 8)

This is not to say that the Christian will not ever commit another sin. What this means, and is translated this way in some modern versions, is that the believer will not *"continue to practice sin."* Sin will no longer be a way of life. The old way is to be put away. We are to have a *"new heart and right spirit"* that clearly shows in the way we live.

There are other problems with this legal / forensic model, but I feel we have presented enough here for you to get the picture. As I mentioned earlier, while there may be situations in which this legal model that may be found beneficial, it certainly has its limitations. What I have presented here may have prompted more questions in your mind. For example, if Jesus didn't die to pay our penalty so God would forgive us, why did He have to die? If God doesn't do it, how is the sinner punished? Is there a better way to define just what sin is? Those questions, as well as many others will be answered in our study of the other models of salvation.

As I mentioned at the beginning of this chapter, the legal model may be suitable as a "beginning model" for some who need it. But it is dangerous to stay in the beginning stage of Christianity all our lives, we are to learn and grow, as the Apostle Peter wrote, *"in the grace and knowledge of Jesus Christ"* (II Peter 3:18). So that we no longer remain "babes in Christ," we need a more advanced model which we discover in the next chapter.

Chapter Four

The Deliverance Model

The next model we will examine is a more advanced model we will refer to as the "Deliverance Model." In this model there is no emphasis on legal matters such as law and judgment, penalties and pardon. In this model, God is still seen as possessing enormous power as Sovereign Creator and Ruler of the universe. He is perfectly good and righteous, concerned only with the welfare of His creatures. But in this model God has an enemy, a rebellious angel once called Lucifer, who by subtlety spreading deceptive lies about God caused the defection of a third of the angels in heaven. This led to a war in which Lucifer, now called Satan, and his angelic followers were cast out of heaven to the earth where Satan then found great success in deceiving the inhabitants on this planet.

Satan's lies that man has believed have resulted in the selfish, disorderly, and deadly behavior known as sin. And having been taken captive by this cunning and deadly foe, man is powerless to regain his lost freedom. His only hope lies in being rescued from the bondage of this life threatening danger by a power outside himself and God is that deliverer, a Savior who comes to this dangerous world to rescue His children from the captivity of Satan and death. As with the previous model, our first question is: Is this model biblical? To answer we begin in the book of Revelation -

"And war broke out in heaven: Michael and his angels fought with the dragon; and the dragon and his angels fought, but they did not prevail, nor was a place found for them in heaven any longer. So the great dragon was cast out, that serpent of old, called the Devil and Satan, who deceives the whole world; he was cast to the earth, and his angels were cast out with him." (Revelation 12:7-9)

The Dragon, or Satan, is here referred to as *"that serpent of old,"* which brings to mind the time shortly after the creation of the earth when Satan, disguised as a serpent began his work of deception in the Garden of Eden. The text said he *"deceives the whole world."* How did he do that and what was the issue involved? We go back to the garden to find the answer -

"Now the serpent was more cunning than any beast of the field which the LORD God had made. And he said to the woman, "Has God indeed said, 'You shall not eat of every

tree of the garden'?" And the woman said to the serpent,
"We may eat the fruit of the trees of the garden; but of the
fruit of the tree which is in the midst of the garden, God has
said, 'You shall not eat it, nor shall you touch it, lest you
die.' " Then the serpent said to the woman, "You will not
surely die. For God knows that in the day you eat of it your
eyes will be opened, and you will be like God, knowing
good and evil." So when the woman saw that the tree was
good for food, that it was pleasant to the eyes, and a tree
desirable to make one wise, she took of its fruit and ate. She
also gave to her husband with her, and he ate."

(Genesis 3:1-6)

There were two key issues in Satan's conversation with Eve that have had an immeasurable impact on mankind since that day. God said if they ate of the tree of the knowledge of good and evil they would die; Satan said they would not. So the first issue that immediately jumps out at us is that Satan has insinuated that God has lied to them; that God's word cannot be trusted.

And it is true, up to that time in the history of the universe there had been no death. There wasn't anything God could point to and say, "Look at this, this is what death is." At the same time, Satan could testify that he had disobeyed God and remains as alive as ever. Who was Eve to believe? She had no tangible evidence; it was simply Satan's word against God's word.

The second issue is more subtle and thus has been overlooked by many. It has to do with the nature of sin and death. How are we to understand God's statement, *"if you eat of that tree, you will die."* First of all, the Bible says it was the tree of *"the knowledge of good and evil."* Though it may have been a literal tree, it must have also been a symbol, and *"eating"* of this tree represented personally experiencing good and evil, kind of like tasting that banana we mentioned in the first chapter. The real issue is: Did God mean that certain kinds of behavior would result in man's death as a natural consequence; or did God mean that they would be put to death as punishment for disobedience to His command? Was God warning them of a deadly danger, or was He threatening them with the death penalty? Of these two choices, what are we to believe? What is the nature of sin? Do certain types of behavior result in death as a natural consequence? Or is death the penalty imposed upon sinners as punishment for sin? According to our study of the legal model, it would appear that the world is captive to the teaching that death is God's legally imposed punishment for sin.

Now, if that teaching is true, then what if God *did not* punish sinners by putting them to death? Would they still die? The logical answer would be no. If they are not put to death, or executed, there would be no reason for them to die and Satan has told the truth – if you disobey God you won't die, God has deceived us. After careful thought, we must conclude what God said was a warning and not a threat.

Which brings us back to the other issue – Can God be trusted? Can we believe His word? Has the whole world been deceived on this issue too? I think most people would say, of course God can be trusted, no one questions that! We say that, but if that is true, why is there so much disagreement regarding what God's Word actually says? The Catholic priest, the Jewish rabbi, and the Protestant preacher all say they speak for God; all of them say they have the truth; all of them say "the Bible says," yet all of them teach different things. All of them can't be right; all of them can't have the truth. The fact is that some have placed traditional church doctrines and the teachings of the church fathers above God's Word. In doing that it demonstrates they place more trust in man's wisdom and reasoning than they do in the Word of God. As we saw in the last chapter, church history clearly shows that it has happened in the past, and unfortunately not much has changed; it is still a problem today!

All this began with the parents of the human race who were taken captive by the serpent's lies. Adam and Eve believing these lies were changed in ways we could not understand until recently. Today, with the new high-tech devices available to them, brain scientists are learning many things about the brain that couldn't be known before. According to these brain scientists, contrary to what was previously believed, we can actually change our brain. Note the following quotes about the brain from the book, "The Mind and the Brain – Neuro-plasticity and the Power of Mental Force" by Jeffery M Schwartz, published 2002 by Harper.

"The brain, to be sure, is indeed the physical embodiment of the mind, the organ through which the mind finds expression and through which it acts in the world."

(The brain is the "control center" of our being.)

"The function of effort is to keep affirming and adopting a thought which, if left to itself, would slip away....It is the power of attention – to select one possibility over all others – that invests us with an efficacious will. The essential achievement of the will is to attend to one object and hold it clear and strong before the mind, letting all others, its rivals for attention and subsequent action, fade away like starlight swamped by the radiance of the sun."

(In other words, we will retain that to which we give our attention, other things will slip away and be forgotten.)

"Through changes in the way we focus attention, we have the capacity to make choices about what mental direction we will take;"

(Real evidence that God has created man with a free will.)

"More than that, we also change, in scientifically demonstrable ways, the systematic functioning of neural circuitry....Our actions are shaped by our will and our will by our attention....Choice is generated by a persons mind and it changes his brain."

(The words above in parenthesis are mine.)

Note the statement: "Choice is generated by a persons mind and it changes his brain." From this evidence we must conclude, that when Adam and Eve freely made the choice to trust the word of the serpent and disregard the word of

God, new neural pathways were developed which resulted in their brain actually being changed. The frightening part is that they were from that moment taken captive by those changes. The way they saw everything, especially God, was now very different. They once had welcomed His visits "in the cool of the day," but now they hide in fear of Him and sought to cover themselves. When God confronted them, the "blame game" began. Blaming God, blaming each other, blaming the serpent... Something had drastically changed inside their minds, something that only God could rectify. There is a lesson here for us all. If we do not make a consistent, intentional effort to remember God and His ways we will forget, and Satan will fill our minds with other things just as he did with Eve! But if we will make an intentional effort to pay attention to the way of the Lord we will prosper.

"Blessed is the man Who walks not in the counsel of the ungodly, Nor stands in the path of sinners, Nor sits in the seat of the scornful; But his delight is in the law of the LORD, And in His law he meditates day and night. He shall be like a tree Planted by the rivers of water, That brings forth its fruit in its season, Whose leaf also shall not wither; And whatever he does shall prosper."

(Psalm 1:1 - 3)

Clearly we have choices to make that will affect our future, but if we choose to keep doing the same things we've always done, we will keep getting the same results we've always gotten. But changing is easier said than done. There are distractions, some are important, like work and family, but the key is balance, not to let any one of these become all consuming.

Probably the most dangerous distraction for us today is the entertainment media. It has spoiled us with all the excitement, the drama, the wide range of emotions we experience with TV shows, movies, novels and sports. Once we get hooked on that everything else can become pretty boring. How can the Bible, the Church, or the family compete with all the media's hype and excitement? That's a problem and a challenge for most of us. But it does not change the reality that if we are going to change the way we are, we must make an intentional effort – a conscious attempt to change the neural circuits in our brains. It will be kind of like a child going from french fries to turnip greens – a new taste must be acquired, and that will take time and effort! This is part of *"working out our own salvation with fear and trembling"* (Philippians 2:12).

Researchers have also discovered that certain behavior affects the DNA and is thus passed on to the offspring. Alcoholism is an example of this. In the same way, the deadly psychological condition incurred by Adam and Eve in the Garden of Eden has passed through the DNA of every generation since that fateful day as the Apostle Paul confirms in Romans –

"Wherefore, as by one man sin entered into the world, and death by sin; and so death passed upon all men, for that all have sinned."   (Romans 5:12)

In the deliverance model, humans are not born sinners or criminals, but rather born with "brain damage" so to speak. Every human is born captive to a mental condition which produces selfish, sinful behavior. In the biblical languages, the word most often translated *"sin"* simply means, *"to miss the way, to miss the goal, or to miss the path of right."* And what is the goal, or path of right that we miss? The Bible tells us in Romans 3:23 - *"For all have sinned and fallen short of the glory of God."* What is the *"glory of God"* we all have fallen short of? If we go back to the story of Moses we find that he once asked the Lord to show him His glory.

"And he (Moses) said, "Please, show me Your glory." Then He (the Lord) said, "I will make all My goodness pass

before you, and I will proclaim the name of the LORD before you. I will be gracious to whom I will be gracious, and I will have compassion on whom I will have compassion." But He said, "You cannot see My face; for no man shall see Me, and live." And the LORD said, "Here is a place by Me, and you shall stand on the rock. So it shall be, while My glory passes by, that I will put you in the cleft of the rock, and will cover you with My hand while I pass by. Then I will take away My hand, and you shall see My back; but My face shall not be seen:" (Exodus 33:18 – 23)

Notice when Moses asked to see His glory, the Lord said *"I will make all my goodness pass before you."* The Lord put Moses in the cleft of the rock and then –

"And the LORD passed before him and proclaimed, "The LORD, the LORD God, merciful and gracious, longsuffering, and abounding in goodness and truth, keeping mercy for thousands, forgiving iniquity and transgression and sin," (Exodus 34:6)

The glory of God that the Lord wanted Moses to see was not His physical beauty or the brightness of His presence, but rather the *"glory"* of His gracious *"name,"* that is, His gracious character! God's gracious character is what He wants us to behold today that we may be changed into His image, so we may be more like Him. The Bible says -

"For it is the God who commanded light to shine out of darkness, who has shone in our hearts to give the light of **the knowledge of the glory of God in the face of Jesus Christ."** (2 Corinthians 4:6)

"But we all, with unveiled face, beholding as in a mirror the glory of the Lord, **are being transformed into the same image** *from glory to glory, just as by the Spirit of the Lord."* (2 Corinthians 3:18)

The *"glory of God"* is perfectly seen in Christ. But all humans fall short of living and loving as He did. But yet as we *"behold Him"* we are transformed into the same image and become partakers of His gracious nature -

"By which have been given to us exceedingly great and precious promises, that through **these you may be partakers of the divine nature,** *having escaped the corruption that is in the world through lust."* (2 Peter 1:4)

The divine nature is grounded in the fact that *"God is love."* Not the emotion called love, but an unchangeable principal of unselfish concern for others. The Greek word for this kind of love is "agape." When the Bible says "God is love," the word is "agape." This kind of love is not just an attribute of God, but the very nature and essence of God. I have been unable to find a really good definition for the Greek word "agape" in the dictionaries. However, we can find a great description of "agape" in the following verses -

"Love is patient and kind. Love is not jealous or boastful or proud or rude. Love does not demand its own way. Love is not irritable, and it keeps no record of when it has been wronged. It is never glad about injustice but rejoices whenever the truth wins out. Love never gives up, never loses faith, is always hopeful, and endures through every circumstance. Love will last forever."

(1 Corinthians 13:4 - 8 NLT)

Love being the very essence of God's being, these verses should be a description of the nature of God. If we substitute the word *"love"* in these verses with the word *"God,"* notice how it reads:

"God is patient and kind. God is not jealous or boastful or proud or rude. God does not demand His own way. God is not irritable, and keeps no record of it when He has been wronged. God is never glad about injustice but rejoices whenever the truth wins out. God never gives up, never

loses faith, is always hopeful, and endures through every circumstance. God will last forever."

This, I believe, is the true description of our loving Heavenly Father and what He is really like; there is no better place to see that demonstrated than in the life and death of Jesus Christ. The Bible calls this kind of love the *"royal law."*

"If you really fulfill the royal law according to the Scripture, "You shall love your neighbor as yourself," you do well;" (James 2:8)

The word here for love is the same, it is agape'. This is a law because it is a principle based on a reality out of which God made and sustains life which was designed to be governed by the righteous principals of unselfish love.

"For all the law is fulfilled in one word, even in this: "You shall love your neighbor as yourself." (Galatians 5:14)

Love is the principal behind all God's law, and sin is the violation of God's law of love – "missing the way of right," which is the way of love. The Bible also calls sin a law –

"But I see another law in my members, warring against the law of my mind, and bringing me into captivity to the law of sin which is in my members." (Romans 7:23)

Sin is a law because it too, is a principle based on reality. It is not just another way of living which happens to be different from God's way. The problem with sin is not that God doesn't like it, but that sin is wrong. Sin is inherently hurtful and by its very nature is damaging and deadly. The Bible actually calls it *"the law of sin and death."*

"For the law of the Spirit of life in Christ Jesus has made me free from the law of sin and death" (Romans 8:2)

God created the universe to function as a circle of love with Him as the Source. God is the source of life and love and *"every good and perfect gift"* (James 1:17). We receive from Him through Christ and in turn we give to others who then give back to God thus completing the circle of love. Sin is moving out of the circle of receiving and giving, exercising our natural impulse to take and keep. Since selfishness is basically the opposite of love, selfishness is the root of all sin. Name any sin and think it through and you will find that its foundation is selfishness. Its all about "me" - my wants - my needs - my rights!

The truth is, selfishness deceives man with the idea that "looking out for ole number one" is the only way to survive in this world. But this is an illusion that in time often leads to guilt, and guilt leads to blaming others just as Adam and Eve experienced in the beginning. This psychological derangement of the mind chokes out love and exalts self and has been passed down to every human being and all of us are held in captivity to it. The selfish, rebellious behavior that resulted from being taken captive to the lies of Satan has taken deep root in the mind of every human being. As the Apostle Paul realized he was captive to this condition, he cried out to God for deliverance -

*"For I delight in the law of God according to the inward man. But I see another law in my members, warring against the law of my mind, and **bringing me into captivity to the law of sin** which is in my members. O wretched man that I am! **Who will deliver me from this body of death?"***

(Romans 7:22-24)

The Lord has heard the cries of man for deliverance -

*"For He looked down from the height of His sanctuary; From heaven the LORD viewed the earth, **To hear the***

groaning of the prisoner, To release those appointed to
death,"   (Psalm 102:19- 20)

When the time was right, God in the person of Jesus Christ came as the Deliverer, the Savior of the world –

"Inasmuch then as the children have partaken of flesh and blood, He Himself likewise shared in the same, that through death He might destroy him who had the power of death, that is, the devil, and release those who through fear of death were all their lifetime subject to bondage."
                                                (Hebrews 2:14,15)

In the deliverance model, Jesus did not die to "pay for our sin," or to legally justify God in forgiving us, but rather to expose the lies of Satan which have had such a detrimental impact on us all. Satan was unmasked at the cross; his lies about God were exposed at Calvary while all our questions about God's love, His trustworthiness, and the nature of sin and death are answered at the cross.

Remember the questions presented at the outset of this chapter. Can God be trusted? Does sin lead to death? Think about the cross; remember Jesus cry, *"My God, My God, why have you forsaken me?"* As *"He who knew no sin was made sin for us,"* Jesus sensed He was being separated from God, the source of life. And being "forsaken," being separated from the source of life, Jesus died the sinners death. This is clear evidence that sin does result in death, that God can be trusted; He told the truth – sin is deadly. Sin cuts the sinner off from God, and being cut off from God, in the end the sinner will die as Jesus did – not from crucifixion, but from being separated from the very source of life. (See my book, "Questions at the Cross" for a detailed biblical study on the death of Christ.)

Any doubt or question about God's love for us was also answered at Calvary. During Jesus' suffering of the crucifixion, there was no point at which He could say – "I can't love you any more than this...I've got to take care of myself now...I will come down from the cross and return to my Father." No, God's love knows no bounds, it is truly *"stronger than death!"* (Sing of Solomon 8:6). The truth that frees us is clearly revealed at Calvary.

"Then Jesus said to those Jews who believed Him, "If you abide in My word, you are My disciples indeed. And you shall know the truth, and the truth shall make you free."

(John 8:31-32)

The truth about God's character of love will deliver the mind that is being held captive by Satan's lies.

Note the following texts -

*"And a servant of the Lord must not quarrel but be gentle to all, able to teach, patient, in humility correcting those who are in opposition, if God perhaps will grant them repentance, so that **they may know the truth, and that they may come to their senses and escape the snare of the devil, having been taken captive by him** to do his will."*

(2 Timothy 2:24-26)

*"Casting down arguments and every high thing that exalts itself against the knowledge of God, **bringing every thought into captivity to the obedience of Christ,"***

(2 Corinthians 10:5)

*"There is therefore now no condemnation to those who are in Christ Jesus, who do not walk according to the flesh, but according to the Spirit. **For the law of the Spirit of life in Christ Jesus has made me free from the law of sin** and death."*

(Romans 8:1-2)

The following is a clear and logical explanation by Dr Tim Jennings M.D., psychiatrist, of how this works -

"A critical principle to recognize is that only by seeing, comprehending, and recognizing the truth about God's character, is it possible to experience grace and truth. It is through the avenue of "seeing" the truth about God that wins us to trust and opens the mind to the working of the Holy Spirit. In other words, it is by "seeing" the truth about God, as revealed in Jesus, that we receive God's healing grace and truth. Those who reject the truth about God's character of love, those who accept a different version of God's character – such as a stern judge, one who inflicts eternal penalties etc. obstruct the experience of God's grace and truth, for it is by seeing His glory that we are healed.

The Bible is teaching more than just a change in cognitive understanding or psychological reorganization. What we believe has power over us, power to heal and power to destroy. When we see the truth about God, believe that truth, internalize that truth the change in understanding causes a change in brain function. The anterior cingulate cortex (ACC), where we experience love, compassion, empathy, other-centered regard, grows stronger as we see, meditate and comprehend the character of God as revealed in Jesus. This growth corresponds with increased sense of peace and wellness, reduced firing of the brain's fear center, reductions in stress hormones and inflammatory factors and better health here and now. Further, these changes result in brain rewiring and alteration in gene expression. We are changed physically, psychologically, emotionally and spiritually when we come into the knowledge of God as revealed in Jesus.

Conversely, god concepts that diverge from the truth Jesus revealed result in damage to the ACC, inflammation of fear circuitry and increased stress response with worsening health. The increased stress response, resulting from holding to lies about God, shuts off the production of brain proteins which keep the brain healthy. Further, white supporting cells are damaged with subsequent damage to neurons. This combined effect results in loss of brain tissue in critical memory regions and reasoning centers of the brain. In other words, holding to wrong God concepts impairs healthy thinking and reasoning. Jesus came to bring us the truth about God. As we accept the truth and reject the lies, we open the heart in trust and participate in God's healing power and experience change in character, biology and psychology and mental efficiency and are prepared to meet Jesus."

You may read the entire article at:
http://comeandreason.com/index.php/media-center/blog-menu/165-how-are-we-changed-by-beholding-god

As we are drawn to, and continue to study the Word of God and the Cross, if we do not resist we will be changed –

*"For the love of Christ compels us, because we judge thus: that if One died for all, then all died; and He died for all, that those who live **should live no longer for themselves**, but for Him who died for them and rose again."*

(2 Corinthians 5:14-15)

At the Cross we witness a love that is beyond our ability to comprehend. A love so infinite, so selfless and so unlike us that we are tempted to deny its possibility. But if we will believe, its existence will be proved by its influence over our own selfishness. In believing that Christ is the revelation of God's love, sin and selfishness will begin to lose its power over us. As our hearts are bathed in the healing light that streams forth from God's love, it awakens within us a love like His and we are rescued, we are delivered from the deadly bondage of sin and self.

I see this model as a great improvement over the legal view. But there is yet another model, not meant to replace this one but to add to it in significant ways. The next chapter we will introduce and examine the healing model.

Chapter Five

The Healing Model

Both the legal and deliverance models of the plan of salvation have their place, and depending on where one is in their spiritual journey, either can be helpful to one's understanding of salvation. But there is yet another model that takes us to an even deeper level of understanding, and that is the "Healing Model." This model is the one used most often by Christ himself, both in His teachings and demonstrated in many of His miracles.

In this model, rather than Judge and Executioner as in the legal model, or Deliverer as in the deliverance model, God is seen as the Great Physician. And sin, rather than being a criminal act, is the symptom of a deadly infection that plagues all mankind. In this model, the suffering and ultimate death of man is not seen as punishment imposed by God, but rather as the natural consequence of the disease of sin itself. But if one has faith in the Great Physician, and carefully follows His directions, he will be healed of this deadly condition, and though he may still sleep the sleep of death, he will be raised to immortality at the coming of Jesus and live with Him forever.

As we begin our examination of this model, our first question is the same as the others; Is this model biblical? Note the following texts:

*"Why should you be stricken again? You will revolt more and more. **The whole head is sick**, And the whole heart faints. From the sole of the foot even to the head, There is no soundness in it, But wounds and bruises and putrefying sores; They have not been closed or bound up, Or soothed with ointment."*   (Isaiah 1:5,6)

*"But He was wounded for our transgressions, He was bruised for our iniquities; The chastisement for our peace was upon Him, And by His stripes **we are healed**."*
                                         (Isaiah 53:5)

*"I said, "LORD, be merciful to me; **Heal my soul**, for I have sinned against You."*   (Psalms 41:4)

*"Heal me, O LORD, and **I shall be healed**; Save me, and **I shall be saved,** For You are my praise."*   (Jeremiah 17:14)

(The last two verses are written in a style known as Hebrew poetry. Instead of ending each sentence with words that rhyme, in Hebrew poetry the second part of the sentence explains, clarifies, or restates what is said in the first part.

73

The writers of both these verses are stating that being saved is like being healed.)

*"For the hearts of this people have grown dull. Their ears are hard of hearing, And their eyes they have closed, Lest they should see with their eyes and hear with their ears, Lest they should understand with their hearts and turn, So that **I should heal them**."* (Matthew 13:15)

*"When Jesus heard it, He said to them, "Those who are well have no need of a physician, but **those who are sick**. I did not come to call the righteous, but **sinners,** to repentance"* (Mark 2:17)

It can be clearly seen that in these verses the spiritual healing of the sin sick soul is likened to the healing of physical disease. In the New Testament Greek, salvation comes from a family of words, the root word being "sozo" which means, *"to save, keep safe and sound, to rescue from danger or, to save a suffering one from perishing, that is, one suffering from disease, to make well, heal, restore to health."* The following texts are examples of the different ways the word "sozo" is translated:

*"And begged Him earnestly, saying, "My little daughter lies at the point of death. Come and lay Your hands on her, that she may be **healed**, (sozo) and she will live."* (Mark 5:23)

"For she said, "If only I may touch His clothes, I shall be made well." (sozo) (Mark 5:28)

*"And they were greatly astonished, saying among themselves, "Who then can be **saved**?" (sozo)* (Mark 10:26)

"Healed, "made well" and *"saved"* all from the one Greek word, "sozo." Depending on the context, these words not only refer to the healing of physical diseases of the body, but often to the spiritual healing of the heart and mind. As seen in the previous deliverance model, sin originated in the mind of Lucifer who then infected a third of the angels in heaven and later promoted its spread to the human race on this earth.

*"How you are fallen from heaven, O Lucifer, son of the morning! How you are cut down to the ground, You who weakened the nations! For you **have said in your heart**: 'I will ascend into heaven, I will exalt my throne above the stars of God; I will also sit on the mount of the congregation On the farthest sides of the north; I will*

75

ascend above the heights of the clouds, I will be like the Most High." (Isaiah 14:12-14)

"You have said in your heart..." that is, in his mind. A person's thinking is not done in the organ that pumps blood throughout the body as the ancients believed, but in the brain or mind. And as we discussed previously, when Adam and Eve listened to the serpent and then made the deliberate decision to follow his deceptive suggestions their brains were literally changed. Note the following statement from the book, "The New Brain, How the Modern Age is Rewiring Your Mind" by Richard Resak, M.D. pub. by Rodale 2003.

"We now recognize that our brain isn't limited by considerations that are applicable to machines. Thoughts, feelings, and actions, rather than mechanical laws, determine the health of our brain. Furthermore, we now know that the brain never loses the power to transform itself on the basis of experience, and this transformation can occur over very short intervals."

Dr. Resak says here that the brain can transform itself, and that change can occur over very short intervals. When God created Adam and Eve they were created with their minds "wired" for righteousness. But when the serpent introduced the new thought to their minds that God could not be trusted, that He did not have their best interests in mind, and they made the deliberate decision to eat of the tree which God said not to eat of, their brains were "rewired" so to speak and they began to think differently. As a result, they had alienated themselves from God and if He had not come to them and intervened on their behalf, they would not have survived the damage they had done to themselves. One Bible scholar put it this way:

"Man was originally endowed with noble powers and a well-balanced mind. He was perfect in his being, and in harmony with God. His thoughts were pure, his aims holy. But through disobedience, his powers were perverted, and selfishness took the place of love. His nature became so weakened through transgression that it was impossible for him, in his own strength, to resist the power of evil. He was made captive by Satan, and would have remained so forever had not God specially interposed."

(God's Amazing Grace, E. G. White)

"Selfishness took the place of love." And where did that happen? In the mind. This becomes clear as we realize every child is born with the inherited trait of selfishness.

77

Things like greed, hatred, jealousy, lying, stealing, adultery, violence, murder – all are simply symptoms of the greater psychological disorder of selfishness. And if not checked, this psychological disorder, like cancer, spreads and grows until it consumes its victim and in the end, completely destroys him!

Most of us have seen enough in life to know this. So why do we cling to it – why do we try to justify it? Have we convinced ourselves that we are fine just as we are – that we have no need to change? Do we think we can continue through life doing the same selfish, sinful things and yet somehow it will come out different for us? That is insane! In fact, that's what sin is – it's insanity!

We can see the parent-child model here as well. If parents have a child who is mentally ill and due to this condition behaves badly, the parents may hate what the child does, but they still love and pity the child realizing he doesn't really know what he's doing. Therefore the parents don't punish the child but do everything they can to help him. This is likely what Jesus had in mind when He said, *"Father forgive them – they know not what they do"* (Luke 23:24).

This model also helps us better understand how God loves the sinner while hating the sin. And more than that, it helps us see how we should relate to others whom we see as great sinners. Instead of judging and condemning, we should love and pity; the worse others are behaving the more it means they need our sympathy and our help, the more they need the Great Physician. Sinners are not criminals; they are sin-sick, and some are much sicker than others and thus need more help.

According to the Bible, we are all from the same parentage. Good or bad, obedient or disobedient, we all are God's children descended from Adam and Eve. In the Bible God's disobedient children are referred to as the "wicked" which we understand that to mean that they are evil, unworthy, and deserving of punishment. But that is the "forensic / legal model" way of thinking. If we were to do a word study on the word "wicked" we would find something interesting. The New Testament Greek word for "wicked" is "poneros" and it means, *"full of hardships – pressed and harassed – **diseased or blind**."* So, in place of "wicked," translators of the Scriptures could correctly have used the word "diseased" instead. God's rebellious children are not necessarily criminal or evil, but they are diseased and blind! But being influenced by the legal way of thinking the translators chose to use *"wicked"* and still do today.

It is important to note that with the healing model the focus changes from "What must we do to be forgiven" to "What must we do to be to be healed – to be made well?" And what must one do to be healed? What is the healing process? First of all, we must realize and admit that we are sick.

*"If we say that we have no sin, we deceive ourselves, and the truth is not in us. **If we confess our sins**, He is faithful and just to forgive us our sins and to cleanse us from all unrighteousness."*   (1 John 1:8,9)

Some people, like the alcoholic in denial, insist that they do not have a problem in spite of their behavior. So the first step, just as with the alcoholic, is that the sinner must admit, or "confess," that they do have a problem – that they are sick! But even then, if they try to correct their behavior by themselves they will ultimately fail. However, once a person is willing to admit that they are sick and realize that they can't heal themselves, they are ready for the next step. Remember Jesus said, *"They that are whole do not need a physician, but those who are sick."*

The next step is to find the right physician. This needs to be done with great care. We don't want to go to a quack, or a doctor who has not been proven to be reliable.

We want to find one with whom we can trust our very life. The Bible tells us who that is -

*"Let it be known to you all, and to all the people of Israel, that by the name of Jesus Christ of Nazareth, whom you crucified, whom God raised from the dead, by Him this man stands here before you whole. This is the 'stone which was rejected by you builders, which has become the chief cornerstone.' Nor is there salvation in any other, **for there is no other name under heaven given among men by which we must be saved.**"* (Acts 4:10-12)

As the Creator, Christ alone can *"create in us a new heart."* He can re-wire our damaged brains. He is the "Great Physician," the only One who can heal us and make us whole. Our prayer now becomes the same as that of King David - *"Create in me a clean heart, O God, And renew a steadfast spirit within me."* (Psalm 51:10) Jesus gives us the simple formula for the process of salvation:

*"But why do you call Me 'Lord, Lord,' and do not do the things which I say? Whoever **comes to Me**, and **hears My sayings** and **does them**, I will show you whom he is like: He is like a man building a house, who dug deep and laid the foundation on the rock. And when the flood arose, the*

stream beat vehemently against that house, and could not shake it, for it was founded on the rock." (Luke 6:46-48)

Note the steps –

1) Come
2) Hear / Listen
3) Do / Co-operate

1) Come: Having chosen our Physician, we must make the effort to come to him. Jesus said, *"the one that comes to me I will by no means cast out"* (John 6:37). But Christ will not force us. If we won't come – He can't help us. We also must faithfully keep our appointments. This includes keeping the Sabbath, daily devotions, Bible study, prayer and witness. If we are too busy and allow other things, even "good" things, to take up our time and there is no time left for treatment, our recovery will be greatly hindered!

2) Listen: We must pay careful attention to what our physician says and what treatments He may prescribe. If we don't, we may misunderstand and do the wrong things. And we should also be careful about listening to what others tell us. Even though they may have good intentions, they may not give us the counsel that will produce healing.

3) Do - Cooperate: Everyone wants to be well – to be saved, but some don't want to do what the doctor says. But in order for us to get well, we must co-operate with our physician. The doctor may say we need a little surgery, or we may need to get some exercise or take some medicine. If we won't go, if we won't keep our appointments, if we won't listen or refuse to do what the doctor prescribes, how can we expect to get well? This is where faith and trust come in.

Doctors cannot save their patients who do not trust them, who do not have enough faith in them to keep their appointments and do the things they prescribe. Somehow they believe they know better than the doctor. Doctors may love their sick patients; they may forgive them for not taking their medicine, but love and forgiveness on the doctor's part will not heal the disease.

The Bible says God has *"Loved you with an everlasting love"* (Jer. 31:3) and that *"His mercy endures forever"* (Ps 118:1). But if we harden our hearts and will not listen; if we will not be careful to follow His instructions, He will still forgive and love us, but He can't heal us – He can't save us! That means, if we don't study God's Word – if we don't pray to connect with God – if we don't love truth, if we don't do the things the Bible says we should do that enhance our relationship with God, the healing changes our brains need will not take place; our characters will not be changed; the cancer of sin will not go into remission and we will perish. Ultimately, we are either in the recovery process and our sinful condition is in remission, or we are getting sicker and closer, not only to physical, but to spiritual death as well.

In the healing model, God does not stand as the executioner of the sentence against the wicked just as medical doctors do not kill their diseased and dying patients. They do everything possible to heal and save them! In the same way, God, the Great Physician does not kill His sick and dying children either! No, rather than condemning us God is trying desperately to save us – not so He won't have to punish us, but rather to prevent sin from destroying us! *"For the wages of sin is death, but the gift of God is eternal life in Christ Jesus our Lord."* (Romans 6:23) *"...and sin, when it is full grown, brings forth death."* (James 1:15)

Let me emphasize again, we must trust and co-operate with the Great Physician or healing will not take place and eventually we will be so hardened in sin that we will become incurable and God will have to *"give us up"* to the horrible consequences of the second death.

I have heard some make the comment regarding this model that it is legalistic because it calls for us to be careful to follow God's directions. But if God is as we believe and how the Bible presents Him to be, the very essence of love and compassion, righteous, all-wise, all knowing – having only our best interests in mind, if God is all this and He says we should do this or do that and not do the other, it is not legalism to do what He says, it just makes good sense! Moses said it rightly: *"And the* LORD *commanded us to observe all these statutes, to fear the* LORD *our God, for our good always, that He might preserve us alive, as it is this day."* (Deuteronomy 6:24)

God gave His Law for our good always, not to keep us in bondage to Him but to free us to live forever! In the next chapter we will look at perfection in light of the healing model.

Chapter Six

Perfection in the Healing Model

We have seen a progresion of sorts as we have moved from the legal model to the deliverence model and finally to the healing model. The healing model results in just that, complete healing or one might even say perfection. But then, most everyone believes that to think of any human being as perfect is unrealistic. But before we dismiss this thought lets look at what the Bible says about perfection. We will begin this study by looking at some verses from the King James Version -

*"And when Abram was ninety years old and nine, the LORD appeared to Abram, and said unto him, I am the Almighty God; walk before me, and **be thou perfect**."*

(Genesis 17:1 KJV)

*"**Thou shalt be perfect** with the LORD thy God."*

(Deuteronomy 18:13 KJV)

*"There was a man in the land of Uz, whose name was Job; and **that man was perfect** and upright, and one that feared God, and eschewed evil."* (Job 1:1 KJV)

*"Finally, brethren, farewell. **Be perfect**, be of good comfort, be of one mind, live in peace; and the God of love and peace shall be with you."* (2 Corinthians 13:11 KJV)

*"Therefore **you shall be perfect**, just as your Father in heaven is perfect."* (Matthew 5:48 NKJV)

If it is not possible for a person to be perfect, then why has the Lord commanded it? If Jesus has told us to do it, shouldn't we take it seriously? Could it be that once again there is a misunderstanding of the biblical word used? What did Jesus mean when he said we are to be perfect?

If we go to the original languages of the Bible and examine the word *"perfect"* we find the Hebrew word translated *"perfect"* is "tamin" and the Greek is "telios." Both of these words mean to be "mature," to be "complete" or to be "whole." Complete as in a work that has been finished – whole as complete with nothing missing and mature as being fully grown, fully developed. Fortunately most modern translations use these words instead of "perfect" thereby eliminating many misunderstandings about perfection.

When we visit our physician with a troublesome ailment, we want *complete* recovery. It would be ridiculous to think since *"nobody can be perfect"* – that we would only hope to get a little better. And when it comes to spiritual healing, the Bible teaches complete recovery.

"Being confident of this very thing, that He who has begun a good work in you will complete it until the day of Jesus Christ." (Philippians 1:6)

Jesus will "complete" the work he has begun in us. So when the Lord says, *"you shall be perfect"* - He is saying to his followers, *"you are to grow-up – you are to be mature – you are to be complete, nothing missing."* God does not want us to stay "babes in Christ" all our lives, *"tossed to and fro and carried about by every wind of doctrine"* (Ephesians 4:14) and needing someone to take care of us all the time.

It's sad that God's offer of perfection, of complete recovery or total healing is seen by many as a legalistic requirement impossible to obtain. But after taking a closer look at the Word of God, we see that perfection is a precious promise to those who need God's spiritual healing. Perfection is not a command; we are not asked to heal ourselves, but Jesus asks us, just as he did the paralytic at the pool… *"Would you like to be made whole?"* (John 5:6) The Great Physician, God himself, has offered to make us completely whole, to completely heal all the damage done by sin. But we must cooperate. We must consistently put ourselves in the place where the Holy Spirit can heal and transform us that we may become more and more Christ-like. Those who do this are safe to save – no matter how much healing or growth may be needed to reach their final goal. This is vital for the Christian living in the end times. The Bible says –

*"That we should no longer be children, tossed to and fro and carried about with every wind of doctrine, by the trickery of men, in the cunning craftiness of deceitful plotting, but, speaking the truth in love, **may grow up in all things into Him who is the head--Christ--**from whom the whole body, joined and knit together by what every joint supplies, according to the effective working by which every part does its share, causes growth of the body for the edifying of itself in love."*   (Ephesians 4:14 – 16)

I am not sure that many of us will reach God's ideal in this life, but as long as we are growing, as long as we choose to remain in the healing process, God will complete it when Jesus comes again. Remember what we read in a previous chapter from the book of Corinthians – *"At the last trump... this corruption will put on incorruption."*

So we can conclude that *"you shall be perfect"* is not a command but rather a generous offer to each of us. The promise to us is that if we let the Lord have His way, if we will cooperate, we will grow up, we will be made whole. Then it will be safe for us to live with saints and angels in the earth made new!

All of the models of salvation we have studied can be useful, but only if they are not taken beyond their limits and only if they do not distort the truth about God. In fact in all our attempts to teach and witness, we must be very careful we do not "bear false witness" about our Heavenly Father by mis-representing His gracious character. In the final chapter of this book we will discuss why our picture of God and His gracious ways are so vital to our salvation.

Chapter Seven

The Conclusion

As we stated in the closing of the previous chapter, all the models of salvation we have studied can be beneficial, but only if they are not taken beyond their limits and only if they do not distort the truth about God and His gracious character. I believe God and His gracious ways should be the focus of all our doctrines. But of all the many doctrines taught in churches today, I have never heard of a church doctrine specifically focused on the nature and character of God. A church teaching that says – God is like this...." It seems most church doctrine is focused on the church rather than God Himself. But in spite of this unfortunate oversight, I believe the most important topic we can study today in the Church is the truth about the character of God. This important for two reasons:

First – Knowing the truth about God's character will safeguard us from the unintentional worship of a false Christ. Jesus warns us, *"For false christs and false prophets will rise and show great signs and wonders to deceive, if possible, even the elect."* *(Matthew 24:24).*

Many believe that one day near the end of time, in addition to an anti-Christ appearing as some charismatic, powerful human being who will openly oppose God and rule the world, that Satan will appear, "in the flesh" so to speak, claiming to be Christ himself. In fact, the word "anti-Christ" in the biblical Greek is "antee-Christos" which means "in place of Christ." The word itself implies one will come "in place of" Christ, claiming to be Christ. The Bible speaks to this in 2 Thessalonians -

"And then the lawless one will be revealed, whom the Lord will consume with the breath of His mouth and destroy with the brightness of His coming. The coming of the lawless one is according to the working of Satan, with all power, signs, and lying wonders,"   2 Thessalonians 2:8,9

Notice there are two *"comings"* mentioned here. One is the coming of the Lord, but the other is the coming of the lawless one, the anti-Christ. Satan, having superhuman powers, will be able to *"perform great signs and wonders"* the likes of which the world has never seen. The majority of the world will believe that he is Christ; believing that the miraculous things he is able to perform can only come from Divine power. So no matter who comes before that, even someone who appears as a great leader having the ability to unite the world as the anti-Christ is expected to do – ultimately in the end, Satan will be the one who *"sits as*

God in the temple of God, showing himself that he is God." (II Thessalonians 2:4). Make no mistake, Satan is the original and ultimate anti-Christ!

One thing we need to be clear on is that great demonstrations of power and miracles cannot always be trusted as coming from God. Satan can also perform great signs and wonders. But what may be even more dangerous is that with his superhuman intelligence he can twist the Scriptures in such subtle ways that he can easily deceive millions into believing they have the truth when they actually are embracing a lie. But, and this is important to remember, although Satan can deceive with miracles and words, he cannot impersonate God's character of unselfish, unconditional love! That is the very thing that will give Satan away to those who truly know God well. Therefore, only the knowledge of God's true character can be trusted in the last days to distinguish the true Christ from the false and enable one to recognize the impostor!

Second – Knowing the truth about God's character will have an enormous impact on our own nature. The Bible says:

"The idols of the nations are silver and gold, The work of men's hands. They have mouths, but they do not speak;

Eyes they have, but they do not see; They have ears, but they do not hear; Nor is there any breath in their mouths. **Those who make them are like them; So is everyone who trusts in them.** *"*   (Psalms 135:15 - 18)

Did you catch the point of this passage? Those who make the idols and those who trust in the idols will become <u>like</u> the idols! This does not mean that a person will become a statue of wood or granite as those idols were, but it means that the person who worships the idol will develop a character like the character of the god that the idol or statue represents is believed to have.

There is a natural and spiritual law that says, *"By beholding we will become changed into the same image."* That is, over time a person will eventually develop the character and perceived values of the idol, the celebrity, or god they revere and worship. This is known as the "Law of Worship." An example of this human trait is seen in the way many people relate to popular movie stars and sport figures, which ironically are often referred to as "idols." As people become devoted fans of these celebrities many begin to dress like them, talk like them and adopt the same values and worldviews as the one they adore. We were created with the nature of a mirror designed to reflect the spirit of whatever it is we are facing. This same principle applies to the worship of God as we have discussed previously in chapter four -

*"But we all, with unveiled face, **beholding as in a mirror the glory of the Lord, are being transformed into the same image** from glory to glory, just as by the Spirit of the Lord."*   (II Corinthians 3:18)

We have learned that the *"glory"* of the Lord in this context is His gracious character. *"Beholding"* means to observe, to contemplate, to meditate upon. And in this case a person beholding the Lord would begin to develop the same nature or character as the Lord. They would truly come to be more and more like Jesus!

For example, we would not naturally think of loving our enemies because our human nature compels us to hate our enemy. To get even with those who wrong us just seems right, in fact we call it justice. But then as we study the Bible, we read that Jesus says we are to forgive and love our enemies. And more than just telling us what we should do, He also demonstrates it. When we see Christ unselfishly love and forgive his enemies, even dying for them, it awakens something good in us that empowers us to love our enemies too! Jesus is our model of true righteousness. If we are going to idolize any man, it should be the *"Man Jesus Christ"* who, being the *"express image of His person"* (Hebrews 1:3), is the perfect representation of the character of God himself.

So we have two distinct choices before us. One is to behold some worldly idol, person, or system, and become worldly, or we can behold Jesus and become like Him! However, if, because of misunderstanding or false teaching, we develop a false picture of God, we will in a sense then worship a false god. One Bible commentator made the following statement.

"Multitudes have a wrong conception of God and his attributes, and are as truly serving a false god as were the worshipers of Baal." (Review and Herald, E.G. White)

Does this thought help you to see why our picture of God is so critical? What makes the worship of a false god so dangerous for us is that we will develop the character of the god we worship. In the case of the Christian, if we see God as demanding, angry with sinners, condemning and punishing them, then we will likely become demanding Christians who judge and condemn others whom we see as sinners, forgetting we may be the greater sinner by judging and condemning them! You may recall that Jesus said -

"They will put you out of the synagogues; yes, the time is coming that whoever kills you will think that he offers God service." (John 16:2)

Jesus is speaking of certain religious people who have, and will continue to do these things thinking it to be a service to God! In verse 3 Jesus tells us why they do this –

"And these things they will do to you, because they have not known the Father, nor me." (John 16:3)

They do this, not because they are unbelievers, but because of their misunderstanding of God's nature. They actually believe He would approve of such things! They believe that they are simply His instruments to carry out His will.

Does the church today see God in this way? Is He seen as an executioner of the wicked? Unfortunately, after studying the legal model we have to conclude the answer may very well be yes. And the effect that will eventually have on the character of those who see others as hopeless sinners is described in Revelation –

"As many as would not worship the image of the beast should be killed." (Revelation 13:15)

A study in Bible prophecy will reveal that the *"image of the beast"* is a false church - state system that will punish

97

and execute those who oppose it as did the Medieval Church in the Dark Ages and we don't want to be a part of that! So how do we know we are beholding the true God and not some false image? How do we know we have the right picture of God?

We do that by laying aside our pride, our preconceived ideas and opinions, and go to God's Word *"as little children"* with an open, inquisitive mind. If we want to know what God is like, we must study the life and teachings of Christ, who said, *"If you've seen me, you have seen the Father"* (John 14:9).

There are religions today that, while claiming to believe in God, do not accept the truth that Jesus is God. And the tragedy of that is that in rejecting this truth they have no accurate picture of God. Without Jesus we cannot know what God is like and how He would act in this world if He were human like us. We would have no Divine Model to pattern our lives after. History has shown and continues to show that without the true picture of God as seen in Christ, men develop a false picture of God. And worshipping a false god, they will become like that god, rather than becoming like Jesus. I believe this is one reason for the history of violence we have seen in many religions, even Christianity, as well as the continuing violence we see today by those who claim to be believers in God. Just think of what a picture of God terrorists and extremists must have. They believe in a god who will cut your hand off if you steal; hang you if you commit adultery; behead you if you reject his prophets. But on the other hand, if everyone saw God as being just like Jesus, they could find no place for violence against another person, even their enemy.

The Bible gives us a perfect photograph of God, and that is Jesus Christ who came to reveal what the Father, so often misunderstood and lied about, is really like. That is the reason God didn't send an angel, an angel simply could not fully and perfectly portray the character of God, only God could do that, so He came.

I remember seeing a sign hanging in a church classroom years ago that said "Don't get your facts from the snake!" Good Advice! We must be careful we aren't getting our information from that old serpent, Satan. Satan lied about God to the angels in heaven, he lied about God in the Garden of Eden, and Satan has lied about God in the Church! Satan is continually misrepresenting the character of God to the human mind. Today I can't help but wonder how different my life might have been had I been told the truth about sin and death, about why Jesus had to die and about God's gracious character when I was that impressionable eleven year old boy. But fortunately, it doesn't matter how old we are, we are never too old to learn the truth and thus be changed, to be delivered from the bondage of satanic lies and be healed of the deadly virus of sin.

In this book we have looked at the three models of salvation. First, we looked at the legal model where the focus is forgiveness and God is forgiveness personified. Then, we saw in the deliverance model the focus was deliverance, and God is the only One who can deliver us from bondage of sin and death. And finally, we saw in the healing model the focus is on healing and only the Great Physician can heal our sin-sick souls. Only God can provide the life saving cure we all need -

"Nor is there salvation in any other, for there is no other name under heaven given among men by which we must be saved."   (Acts 4:12)

So as we end our study, it is my hope that whoever you are reading these words just now, you will realize that no matter what you've done or how long you've done it, you are forgiven. That no matter how long you have been captive to Satan's lies and the bondage of sin, you can be delivered. And that no matter how sin-sick you are, even thinking you are in a hopeless condition, you can be perfectly healed and one day "when the role is called up yonder," you will be there!

Other resources by Pastor Bill Chambers

Questions At the Cross

A biblical study of the Cross of Christ answering questions such as: Who was Jesus who died? How was Jesus death different? Why did Jesus Have to Die? Who tortured and killed Christ? How are we saved by His death? Can one be save without it? These and more will be answered using only the Scriptures.

Love that Heals

This book examines the differences between the Legal view and the Healing model of salvation, but in addition, it also includes chapters that take a closer look at things like: Dark Speech, The Trinity, The Great White Throne Judgment, The Final End of the Wicked and more.

Sure Word Bible Study

A collection of eighteen study guides that cover topics like: The Basic Principles of Bible study, What is God Like, The Origin of Evil, What Happens at Death, Hell, The Passion of Christ, The Healing Model of Salvation, Baptism, The Church and more.

You may obtain any of these books @ amazon.com either in paperback or on Kindle.

Made in the USA
Charleston, SC
18 January 2014